I0801724

THE GHOSTLY TALES OF SALT LAKE CITY

Published by Arcadia Children's Books
A Division of Arcadia Publishing
Charleston, SC
www.arcadiapublishing.com

First published 2021

Manufactured in the United States

ISBN: 978-1-4671-9823-3

Library of Congress Control Number: 2021938348

Notice: The information in this book is true and complete to the best of our knowledge. It is offered without guarantee on the part of the author or Arcadia Publishing. The author and Arcadia Publishing disclaim all liability in connection with the use of this book.

All images courtesy of Shutterstock.com.

Spooky America

THE GHOSTLY TALES OF SALT LAKE CITY

LAURIE ALLEN, CASSIE ASHTON, KRISTEN CLAY, & NANNETTE GUEST-WATTS

Adapted from *Haunted Salt Lake City*
by Laurie Allen, Cassie Ashton, Kristen Clay, & Nannette Guest-Watts

arcadia
CHILDREN'S BOOKS

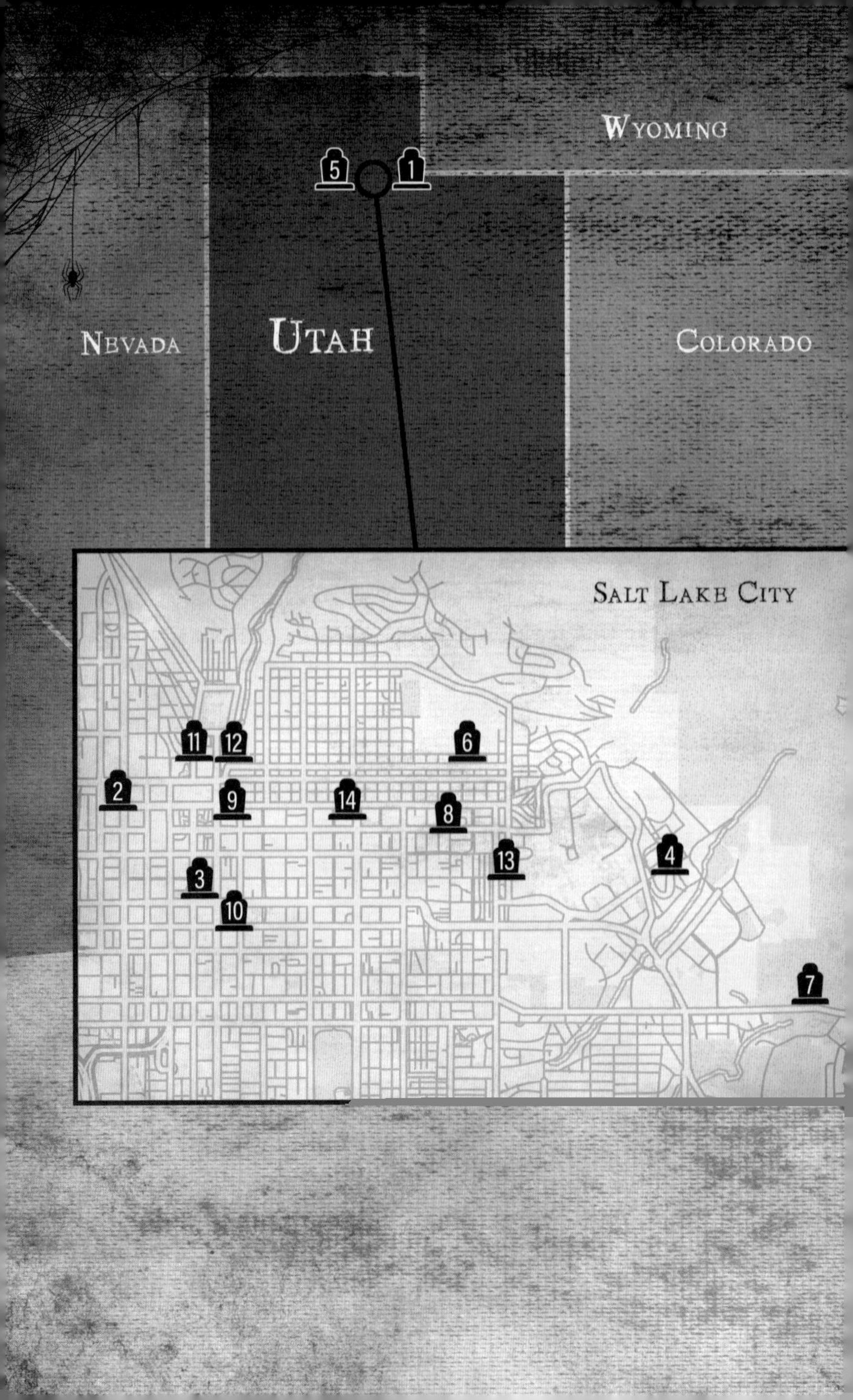
Wyoming
Nevada
Utah
Colorado
Salt Lake City
5
1
11
12
6
2
9
14
8
13
4
3
10
7

Table of Contents & Map Key

Introduction

Have you ever walked by a building and wondered if it was haunted? Have you ever walked by a building *knowing* it is haunted? Storyteller Kristen Clay has. When Kristen moved to Salt Lake City from Hawaii, all the old buildings made her wonder. She thought of the haunted stories she learned in Hawaii and knew these buildings looked haunted.

Kristen was right! Every time she stopped in a building to ask about unseen spirits, a ghost story would come up. She found so many that she that she started Story Tours: Salt Lake City and Ogden Ghost Tours in 2002. She held auditions and hired other storytellers to share the ghostly lore and legends of Salt Lake City.

That is where these stories come from. Generous security guards, custodians, bus drivers, and tour guests shared their haunting experiences. Over time, we even got to know the ghosts ourselves.

We do not attempt to prove the existence of ghosts or try to explain the paranormal. You get to decide whether or not to believe the stories. But we hope to expand your imagination and present you entertainment—and maybe even a chill or two!

In this book, you will experience a sampling of local hauntings and legends. You will learn about Utah Territory, which was a rugged place that drew pioneers fleeing religious persecution. The Latter-day Saints headed west seeking safety and a place to call their own. Their vision was that the desert would blossom as a rose, and it did. The Salt Lake Valley became a safe haven for many others, including miners and businesspeople too. Everyone was welcome.

So, join us on an exciting adventure through Utah's past and back into the present to discover characters who just can't seem to leave this valley, even many years after their deaths. To learn of more adventures, visit www.StoryTours.com.

CHAPTER 1

Vanishing Beauty

In 1847, Brigham Young led a group of pioneers across the Great Plains. Emerging from Emigration Canyon and seeing the barren valley beyond, Brigham declared, “this is the right place.”

Farther down Emigration Canyon, in the middle of a median, you will find a monument to a lone cedar tree. It was one of the few large trees in the valley’s early days. It became a favorite gathering place, especially for the pioneer youth after dancing. Some called it the “Kissing Tree.” Dances were one of the few ways young people could escape the harsh frontier life, so they danced often.

A group of twelve-year-old boys was once on a campout up Emigration Canyon. They huddled in their tent, swapping ghost stories. They passed the flashlight to Martin. It was his turn.

Martin started, "The only ghost story I know happened to Henry, my great-great-grandfather, on Pioneer Day."

"What is Pioneer Day?" asked Quentin.

"Oh, it is a state holiday where we honor the bravery of the first pioneers," August answered.

Martin interrupted, "Guys, listen. It excited Henry to go to the big Pioneer Day dance, hoping he would meet someone new. He was dancing with another girl when he saw her. She was the most beautiful girl he had ever seen. She wore a pretty lavender dress with a matching shawl. He went over and asked her to dance. She said yes. Her name was Marilyn. She was quiet, but her eyes sparkled when she talked to him. They danced all night together. Finally, Henry asked if he could take her home in his horse-drawn buggy. She said yes. Even with her shawl, Henry could tell she was cold. Raised to be a gentleman, he placed his coat around her shoulders to warm her. He asked if she would like to take a long way home. That was code for let's go to the Kissing Tree. She agreed."

"Kissing, oh puke," commented Asher, and they all laughed.

Martin ignored them and continued, "Henry drove to the tree, talking a great deal. He was nervous, wondering what he should do. When they arrived at the tree, it was late and getting stormy. He stopped the buggy and moved closer to her, but before he gathered up his courage, it began raining. Henry knew they had to head home. 'Where do you live?' he asked. She pointed to the south part of town. He

drove the buggy briskly in that direction till they came to a dirt lane. He couldn't see the house; it had no light welcoming her home.

"'Thank you,' she said and hopped down from the wagon and dashed into the darkness. He would've helped her down, but she was fast disappearing down the lane. He couldn't see her, so he went home. It wasn't long before he fell asleep, dreaming of the beautiful girl from the dance.

"The next morning, Henry woke with a smile on his face, thinking about Marilyn. She was in his thoughts all day. He wanted a reason to see her again and remembered. 'She has my coat. She got down so fast I didn't get my coat back. I'll go pick it up.' Henry saddled his horse and rode towards her house.

"Things looked different in daylight. Henry thought he had the right place, but no one lived in the house he thought she entered. They had deserted it a long time ago. Weeds completely covered the yard. It was a mess. He worried. This can't be right. I must be mistaken. Perhaps it was a different street. But no, surely this was where he left her. This was the right house, except that it was empty. Abandoned.

"Baffled, Henry knocked on the door of the closest neighbor. As the door opened, he asked, 'Does a pretty girl named Marilyn live nearby?'

"'Lavender?' questioned the old man at the door. 'Yes, she did. But you don't seem old enough to have known her.'

"'Known her? What do you mean?' puzzled Henry.

"'Lavender died ten years ago of pneumonia. In the winter of '49. She was about your age when she passed. She was pretty—the best dancer in the valley. It was sad. She didn't even live long enough to get a new dress. She only had one good lavender dress. That's how she got her nickname, "Lavender," because of the dress she always wore. You can visit her. She's buried up in the City Cemetery, at the far east end.'"

"Shocked and confused, Henry couldn't believe it. Marilyn, dead! He couldn't think of what else to do, so he rode up to the east end of the Salt Lake City Cemetery. He found her headstone. It read 'Marilyn Watson' and below that, her nickname 'Lavender,' the date of her birth, and her death, dated ten years earlier.

"The eeriest thing he saw, which made the hair on the back of his neck stand up, was on her grave, folded neatly, was his coat. The coat he had wrapped around her shoulders."

"What!" Asher shouted.

"Wait, was she a ghost?" asked August.

"Can you dance with a ghost?" wondered Quentin.

"I don't know," Martin responded. "All I know is my dad said his great-grandpa always swore he danced with the prettiest girl that night dressed in lavender and never saw her again. It was a dance he would never forget."

CHAPTER 2

The Party That Never Stops

Todd, the security guard, walked to the Devereaux Mansion in Salt Lake City and stopped at the front door. All the lights were on, and he could hear dishes being used. He heard laughing and talking. Though he couldn't understand what was being said, it sounded like a party.

He touched the doorknob and started into the house. Everything went dark. No sounds were heard. *That* was normal. There wasn't supposed to be a party there that night. The sounds inside were not coming from any living person.

The Devereaux House was built in 1857. Many fancy parties were held there, as it was the first mansion built in the Utah Territory. The mansion is known for hosting the meeting that kept the peace when General Albert Johnston's army was coming. The US government wanted to make sure that people in Utah were not going to cause problems. Members of The Church of Jesus Christ of Latter-day Saints were afraid there would be persecution and trouble, as there had been in Illinois and Missouri when they had been attacked by mobs for their beliefs. At this meeting, the groups were able to talk and resolve the problems peacefully.

The area became more industrial when the railroad was built. The house was used for other purposes and eventually became run down.

Mrs. Shober, who lived in the home as a teenager, said, "I always thought it was haunted, especially in the living room. I felt like someone's presence was in there."

The house was almost torn down in 1978. In 1979, a fire destroyed parts of the home, and it was abandoned. It has now been restored to its former beauty.

When the Chart House Restaurant opened there, mysterious things started happening. Some people would lose money, keys, or credit cards. After searching through the area, these things would always be found in a cabinet. This cabinet was one of the pieces of furniture in the original house.

A child has been seen sitting on the stairs. When someone mentions that and looks at the stairs again, the child is gone.

The home, now owned by The Church of Jesus Christ of Latter-day Saints, is used for special events. One night, Todd looked at the house. "The lights are on again! Is there a party there tonight?"

"Nothing's on the schedule," replied Andrew, the new guard. "They should be turned off."

"It doesn't do any good," said Todd. "They just turn them back on."

"Who?"

"The ghosts. At least I think that's what's happening there."

"You mean the place is haunted?"

"It's the only explanation."

"Have you seen any ghosts?"

"They disappear when I enter. They don't want me crashing their parties. I did see figures moving on the security camera several times. They're gone when I go into the house."

"Aren't you afraid to go in? I would be!" said Andrew.

"No, they like me. Some guards' keys won't work in the doors, but my keys do."

"Maybe I took the wrong job!" said a panicked Andrew.

"Don't worry. If we don't mess up their parties, they're friendly." Todd left. He turned off the lights and was in the hall near the kitchen when he heard pots and pans rattling. "I was just there. I'd better check again." He walked into the kitchen and everything was still in place. Locking the door, he left the house dark.

He got back to the office and looked—all the lights were on again! He decided it wasn't worth it to turn off the lights.

After their shift, Andrew looked at the house and saw that it was dark. "What's happened? You haven't been back there, have you?"

"No," Todd replied. "The ghosts turn off the lights when their party is over."

Andrew decided to find another job—one without ghosts!

It seems that some people don't want the fun to end. The living aren't invited to these parties. Everything stops when they enter. But you wouldn't want someone to crash your party, would you?

CHAPTER 3

Who Spilled the Beans? And the Spanking Specter of Whiskey Street

A lightning storm had lit up the skies most of the afternoon and by evening had ended. The electricity lingering in the air was still palpable. Kristen and Nannette spent the evening on Whiskey Street gathering stories. Little could they have imagined what was in store for them this ominous September night.

Wanting to get home before the "haunting hour," they stopped at Whiskey Street Cocktails and Dining. They asked about the hauntings and the extra-spectral kitchen at the restaurant.

"Who spilled the beans!?" the irate chef shouted at the staff. "I had an entire pot of chili cooking on the stove, and now look!"

The entire pot of fresh homemade chili had splattered all over the floor. The fact that nobody would admit to the misdeed heightened the chef's rage even more. With a last threat to fire the culprit, he viewed the security footage, but he could not believe his eyes. He called the staff over to make certain of what he was seeing. The pot was sliding inch by inch all by itself! Then it crashed to the floor.

When it comes to food, everyone is a critic—even ghosts. They had a poltergeist! Now, at the discovery of a mess, no one blames the staff. When they view the security footage, they now identify the invisible culprit.

Upon entering the kitchen to start food prep for the day, the staff stood shocked. Video footage showed a bottle of Sriracha sauce being knocked off the shelf by an invisible being, flying across the room, and shattering on the opposite wall.

Nannette and Kristen shuddered at the stories. Before they left, they agreed: a pit stop to the ladies' room was a must.

Chills ran up their spines as they approached the lavatory. However, "When ya gotta go, ya gotta go!" The women were not to be deterred from reaching their destination. Nannette pulled the door open, and the two stepped inside. Both feeling unsettled, they resolved to hurry. As they chatted, the two attempted to ignore their fright.

Kristen stepped out of her stall first. She was washing her hands when, Smack! Someone whacked her on the behind! Incredulous, she turned around. She thought it must have been the stall door that bonked her, but the door was closed.

The hair on her arms rose, and she hesitated in disbelief. Looking around once again and shivering, she called to Nannette. "Um, Nannette, um, a ghost just slapped me on the behind. We need to get out of here!" she stammered.

The ladies then ran from the bathroom as fast as they could and never looked back!

CHAPTER 4

The Ghost and the Girl Scouts

Before selfies, families came to the Fort Douglas Military Museum and asked the staff to take pictures of them posing with "the guy in the Civil War costume." They saw "the guy" leaning against a post on the museum porch, smoking a pipe. Visitors don't believe the staff when they try to explain that there is no costumed character on site. When guests step back onto the porch or look over their shoulder, or out the window, they are often chilled to the bone. There is no trace of the pipe-smoking soldier. The knowledgeable staff then offer the confused family a tour and share the history of the fort.

Camp Douglas's military garrison was set up in 1862. Fort Douglas, as it was later called, is on the East Bench overlooking Salt Lake City. The military entered the Utah Territory to guard the Overland Mail Route, Pony Express, and telegraph lines, as well as to monitor large groups of pioneers entering the territory.

The museum complex is in the historic area of Fort Douglas. It is the favorite haunt of Clem, a well-loved yet mischievous ghost.

Clem, the bearded, pipe-smoking ghost, wears a post–American Civil War uniform. Museum specialists believe Clem was stationed at Fort Douglas after 1865. They believe he worked in the livery stable. That is the area where he is most frequently spotted.

One late spring evening, a full busload of Girl Scouts stopped by the museum as part of a ghost tour.

The girls and their leaders listened with excitement to the guide, Kris. She regaled them with stories of Clem and other ghostly visitors. With a mix of trepidation and giddiness, the Scouts and their chaperones disembarked the bus to explore. The guide stationed herself at the top of the museum complex. Kris watched the group. She hoped they would not disrupt the students prepping for finals in the nearby university housing. She did not want them to attract the scrutiny of security with their mix of giggles and shrieks. Kris's apprehension and constant scanning were unwarranted. The group conducted themselves with good manners, and the tour went on without a hitch. Or did it?

Early the next morning, Kris received a call at home, waking her from slumber. It was Shanice, one of the Girl Scout leaders. With a tremor in her voice, Shanice asked, "Did you hire that Civil War guy? You did, didn't you? I'm sure you did!"

"What?" Kris responded with a sleep-deprived voice.

"I know you guys are pulling a trick on me! The Civil War guy, he was a plant, right?" Shanice pleaded, "You hired him!"

Now more awake and realizing something had happened the night before, Kris sat up in her bed with a jolt and asked the leader to tell her what had happened.

Shanice explained that as they stood on the edge of the porch watching the girls, a man in a Civil War uniform appeared below. He was in the driveway between the two buildings. He stood there, tipped his hat, and waved and blew kisses at her. She giggled and pointed him out to the other two leaders standing with her.

They said, "What guy?"

"That guy right there, the one waving at us and winking!" Shanice insisted.

"I don't see anyone down there," they both maintained.

At the end of the tour, the ladies regrouped with their carpool. Once again, Shanice mentioned the Civil War soldier, and once again, her friends denied seeing him. The hair rose on the back of her neck. Chilled through and through, goosebumps covered her arms. In desperation, she begged them to stop teasing her. They continued their denial.

"Why can't they just admit it? Why can't they let me in on the joke?" Shanice thought. Even her very own daughter seemed to be in on the gag. She tossed and turned all night, pondering what she had seen.

So, at 6:30 in the morning, Shanice woke Kris, hoping to put an end to the caper.

Kris now had shivers up her spine! She replied, "I don't know how to tell you this, but you met Clem!"

CHAPTER 5

Ghost of the Ghastly Grave Robber, and I See Ghosts

Fact is stranger than fiction when one considers the bizarre history surrounding the Salt Lake City Cemetery in the late 1800s.

The early days were not kind to the cemetery, set on a hilltop in the Salt Lake Valley in 1847. Scandal rocked the graveyard only a decade after incorporation. One of the original grave diggers, Jean (John) Baptiste, was the focus of the disgrace. The macabre deeds of Baptiste might have gone undiscovered if it had not been for a Wild West shootout between outlaws and the sheriff.

Hoodlums beat up the disreputable, federally appointed territorial governor, John W. Dawson. They drove him out of town and killed three vigilantes, including Moroni Clawson. No one claimed the bodies, so they were taken to Salt Lake City Cemetery and buried in the potter's field. After hearing of his brother's death, George Clawson came to claim his brother's body and have it moved to the family plot.

Accompanied by Sheriff Henry Heath, George had his brother's body exhumed. Sick by what he saw upon opening the coffin, George screamed!

Sheriff Heath stared into the open coffin in dismay. The sight dumbfounded him. Moroni Clawson was stark naked! It appeared that he was tossed into his coffin carelessly, even though Sheriff Heath had bought a suit for Moroni with his own money before the burial!

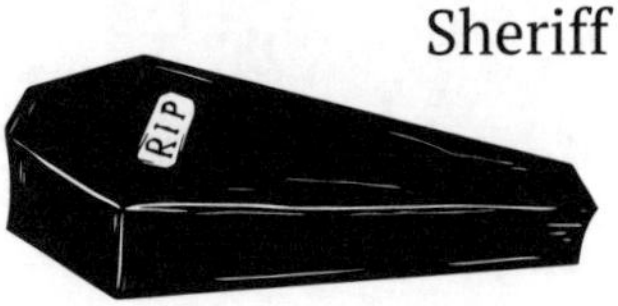

They began an investigation. Bewildered by the reports, a man named Sexton Little suggested they visit the gravedigger, Jean Baptiste. He knew the most about the graves.

Suspicion of Jean Baptiste arose after Sherriff Heath visited his home. Baptiste's wife invited Heath into her home with a sweet expression. While inquiring where her husband might be, he noticed boxes piled around. Glancing into open boxes triggered astonishment—they were full of burial clothes!

Sheriff Heath and his deputies hid at the cemetery. They saw Baptiste pushing a wheelbarrow toward an open grave. In the wheelbarrow lay a naked corpse. Nearby, a bundle of clothes hid in the bushes. Baptiste had been robbing the graves!

They took Baptiste to the Salt Lake City Jail. His fellow inmates wanted to hang him when they recognized the clothes he was wearing—a suit belonging to a saloonkeeper who died and was buried wearing it only weeks before.

Police returning to Baptiste's house shed light on his gruesome deeds. The cellar contained a large vat used to boil the clothes of the sickly dead. They discovered boxes of men's, women's, and children's clothes, along with shoes, jewelry, and watches.

He had robbed over three hundred graves! He only confessed to robbing a dozen in fear for his life.

Anger toward John Baptiste grew. A mob gathered outside the jail and demanded frontier justice. Leaders decided the best punishment would be exile.

West of Salt Lake City lies the Great Salt Lake, the largest saltwater lake in the United States. Banishment to an inhabitable island seemed perfect. The leaders selected Fremont Island, only accessible by boat and used as a cattle post.

They backed a delivery wagon for dairy supplies up to the jail. The sheriff slipped John Baptiste in the back. Unbeknownst to the mob, his exile began. They left him alone with only cattle and wildlife as his companions, a few supplies, and a small shelter.

Three weeks later, deputies went to deliver supplies. There was no trace of John Baptiste. Only the carcass of a cow, a tanned hide, and a dismantled shelter. It appeared he made a raft to escape. They assumed he drowned or died in his escape. He was never seen again.

Or was he?

Individuals in recent years have reported seeing a man carrying a wet bundle of clothes along the south shores of the Great Salt Lake and on Antelope Island. Others report an orb on their cameras and videos in the same locations.

Hoping to get a glimpse of a spirit, ghost hunters peek into the wrought iron opening of the tomb of Jacob Moritz, also referred to as Emo's Grave.

To understand the ghost, you must know who he was in life.

Born in Germany in 1849, Jacob Moritz sought

his fortune in America at the age of seventeen. After working in New York, Milwaukee, and Montana, he made his way to Salt Lake City. He started the Salt Lake Brewing Company in 1883, becoming the most successful brewer in the West.

He and his wife, Lahela, members of the B'nai Israel congregation, engaged in many service and leadership opportunities, often in competition with a fellow congregant, Simon Bamberger.

Jacob Moritz ran for political office against Simon Bamberger. The election was a heated one! Bamberger was well known for an amusement park right in the middle of his railroad line. Moritz was receiving bad press regarding his saloons.

A newspaper called Moritz a "poisonous jimsonweed" and Bamberger an "oak tree." Who do you think won the election after that?

Bamberger! He became the first Jewish governor of Utah and the third Jewish governor in the United States. It devastated Moritz.

Jacob's health failed in 1909. He and Lahela

sailed for Europe hoping rest and the mineral baths of Wiesbaden, Germany, would heal him. But, alas, he died of stomach cancer.

Lahela returned to Utah with his ashes in a black marble vase. She laid him to rest in 1910 in the Israel B'nai Cemetery portion of the Salt Lake City Cemetery. The tomb was large, monumental, made of metal and stone.

The name Emo remains a mystery. How the legends started is a guess.

After legends of Emo grew, many made pilgrimages to the grave. In a dark turn, vandals destroyed the beautiful black marble vessel that once held his ashes. The cemetery moved his ashes to a secret location, hoping he could rest in peace. The cemetery staff placed sheet metal over the opening, sealing it off from unappreciated tokens. Has Jacob Moritz found the rest and peace he sought?

"My grandma sees ghosts . . . and so do I," eleven-year-old Maya announced to the guide at the beginning of the tour.

It was before dusk at the cemetery. The group gathered in front of the tomb. The name MORITZ was emblazoned along the top. Although it was still light out, imaginations grew with curiosity over an iron door. Inside the window stood remains of a beautiful black marble vase.

The guide, Nan, called the group to attention. All eyes widened as she told the story of Jacob Moritz, business leader, electoral embarrassment, servant to the community, and last his death. She pointed across from Moritz's tomb to the grave of his rival, Bamberger. Could Moritz rise from his grave because his enemy is buried right across from him? Imagine being buried face-to-face with your rival. For nine decades, people describe seeing a face with glowing eyes looking out from the iron bars.

Nan invited the group to reenact the ritual of Emo's Grave. With a candle in hand, Jenny, a brave twelve-year-old, walked backward, guided by her friend. They circled the tomb. They chanted, "Emo, Emo, Emo." The third time around, Jenny glanced into the darkness.

"I see something!" Maya called out, pointing to the opening in the crypt. Nan smiled and acknowledged her.

At the same moment, a camera clicked.

Jenny peered inside, giggling.

"Did you see anything?" her friends pressed.

"No," she replied.

"I saw something!" Maya insisted.

"Woah, check this out!" A woman holding a camera ran over to Nan. "I got it! Look!"

Nan, along with the others, stared at the screen in disbelief. Right where Maya had pointed, a pair of eyes, hot and white, glowered from the darkness of the crypt.

"That's what I saw!" Validated, Maya again stated, "I told you I see ghosts!"

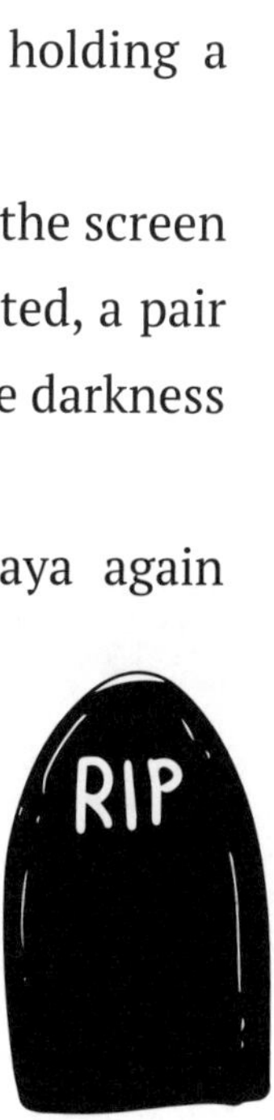

CHAPTER 6

Did You Hear That?

A big white house sits at the crest of a hill in This Is the Place Heritage Park above Salt Lake City. The park is in the location where pioneers first laid their eyes on the Salt Lake Valley below.

Lucy Loomis Tuttle Andrus was a tough pioneer woman. She left England, crossed the plains in a covered wagon, and built a house by herself in 1859. She ran the house and farm as an inn to earn money in a day when women did not do that.

The stars and moon seemed dark, and a misty cloud hung low as Debbi and David approached the house. They were there with their team to do a private tour of the home.

Debbi's skeleton key unlocked the front door and swung it open. The entryway was small, and the stairs leading to the second floor were so close they almost touched the open door.

The group paused as Debbi turned her flashlight off and her camera on. She pointed it up the staircase as the camera flashed through darkness. Debbi looked at the photos. She had something.

No one could see her, but the camera captured her. There was an apparition standing halfway up the stairs. She was translucent, white, in a pioneer dress, carrying a fan in her left hand.

Photo 1: she was coming down the stairs to greet visitors.

Photo 2: she moved her fan up.

Photo 3: she turned her head, looking back upstairs.

This stunned the group. Janene—who was waiting outside—thought the ghost search was successful. She was that close to a real haunted house.

The rest of the group suddenly entered the house! Janene gulped and turned to tell her son they should stay on the porch, but Caden headed through the door smiling.

A gust of cold wind blew leaves, circling toward her. She shivered. Stay outside alone or go inside with people? She entered.

David closed the door, locking them in. Janene's imagination went crazy. Which was worse, being locked inside or out of a haunted house?

She calmed down as Debbi and David told about the inn, a popular stop between Salt Lake City and Provo run by Lucy Andrus. The visitors' dining room was to the right, then the parlor, featuring artwork made by weaving human hair!

The tour continued. On the left, at the back of the house, was the kitchen.

Debbi said there was always activity in the kitchen, but not tonight. Janene gulped.

Lucy had a dry kitchen, meaning there was no water inside the house.

David opened the pantry door as Debbi explained it always has a presence.

Sure enough, the camera captured orbs. Janene could handle orbs—harmless light circles that look like dust specks in a picture. She finally felt calm. Then she glanced at Caden. He looked sick.

She asked if he felt okay. He nodded, but then shook his head. Not okay, but he waved her off. They both looked back at Debbi.

While Debbi was at the house one day, she picked up a wooden bowl that had belonged to Lucy. The minute she did, she felt as if she should not have touched it. She apologized out loud.

Debbi is the only person with a key to this house. The bowl disappeared and was never seen again.

Debbi directed them back into another dining room.

She explained the separate dining rooms for families and for cowboys. She pointed out the wooden floorboards that Lucy installed.

Debbi and the others quickly left the room. Janene turned to Caden to check on him.

He responded that he had felt sick in the kitchen but was fine the minute he walked out that door. He did not think she liked little boys in her kitchen!

They stopped and looked at each other. From the kitchen behind them, they heard footsteps, like boots walking on wooden boards. Caden's wide eyes seemed to say, "Do you hear that?!"

They both had the same idea: get out of here!

Janene heard Caden right behind her as she ran to the front door. Grasping the doorknob, she remembered two things: the front door was locked, and David had the key.

Caden leaped up the stairs, saying Lucy's ghost could not be up there if she was in the kitchen. Janene followed.

The others were already upstairs, in a back bedroom. Debbi took more pictures before they walked out of that room. Straight ahead was another room.

Debbi whispered they would not be going into that room. They kept it locked because Lucy's little boy was afraid of strangers. One rattle of the doorknob, and they would find fresh pee on the bed. Debbi pointed back the way they came.

The group went to the next room, where boarders stayed at the top of the stairs. The group took up most of the hallway while looking in the doorway. Janene's back almost touched the stair rail behind her.

She sensed someone walking up the stairs. You know how you can feel someone there before you see them? She felt that someone wanted to get past them on the stairs and up to the bedrooms.

Janene turned to smile at . . . at . . . air and moved backward against the rail. She sucked in her stomach and reached to pull her son back out of the way too.

The exchange was polite. She caught her breath as she felt, or sensed, the presence pass by.

Caden stared at her. Why did she pull him backward? Too stunned to speak, they both leaned forward to hear Debbi.

Caden asked how everyone fit in that one small room.

David said that cowboys pulled their bedrolls from their horses and rolled them out one beside the other on the ground.

As they prepared to descend the stairway to leave, Debbi said the ghost moved around the house when people toured. True!

Lucy Andrus was quite the hostess—very polite and hospitable. But if you are a young boy, beware of her kitchen.

CHAPTER 7

The Helpful Nuns

The Sisters of the Holy Cross came to Utah in 1875. Father Lawrence Scanlan asked the nuns to take care of Catholic families and miners.

A lot of diseases come from working deep underground without fresh air. The sisters raised money to build a hospital to take care of them. The hospital grew and is now the Salt Lake Regional Medical Center. Some people say the nuns never stopped taking care of patients.

Eliot was a nurse at the hospital for eleven years. He often put other coworkers at ease after their first ghostly encounter. Jake had been standing in the breakroom and felt someone standing over him. No one was there.

Another coworker, Garrick, also had that experience. He and Jake asked Eliot how he stayed so calm with the rumors about Rooms 117 and 118. Eliot knew the stories well.

There had been four patients with two nurses on duty. The call lights kept going on with no patients in those rooms. Sometimes when the nurses went to take vitals on a patient, the patients said the nuns had already been by and took care of them. The nuns offered a drink, extra pillow, or blanket. It happened all the time. The nuns were very helpful, they just did not talk much. The nurses stay quiet about the fact that the nuns haven't been part of the hospital since 1993!

Before the remodel of the old east wing, there were more experiences. Nurses saw nuns flash by, and people saw shadows of them in the old building. The sisters were not as active after remodeling.

If you are hunting for hospital ghosts, just take a visit to Labor and Delivery. They have a ghost nurse who helps in Room 8! Beverly appreciates the help and comfort of the ghost. Would you be calm if a ghost worked beside you?

A lady was in labor in the old east wing in 1995. This mother walked the hallways and then down the stairs. She had a strange feeling, then a nun in full habit passed her on the stairs. She said hello, but the nun did not smile.

These stories did not scare the nurses. The creepy supply room in the basement— called "Materials"— scared Beverly.

A door from the supply room opens right into the morgue. During an autopsy, the doctor blasts classical music. If someone is in Materials, loud music suddenly blares.

If a large man steps out of a doorway, it is probably the security guard, Bill. He does not believe in ghosts.

Bill scoffs at believing in the ghost stories floating around. Bill might be more cocky than confident. He feels his job does not allow for being scared. He thinks he can explain away people's stories.

When Bill was thirteen years old, in 1968, he broke his collarbone. Have you ever broken a collarbone? It's painful! And warranted a visit to the emergency room.

The Holy Cross emergency room used to be in the southwest corner of the building. But hospitals are always changing and expanding. Now the cafeteria is in that area. Can you imagine having lunch in the same place that was once full of blood and broken bones?

Bill knows they cleaned that area when the

cafeteria moved in, but still. Thinking about what it used to be and what it is now could make people think of ghosts. Bill worked security for thirty-four years and never had an experience himself. Yet when six different people told the same ghostly story, it made him wonder.

Patrick was working in the cafeteria storage room. He lifted some heavy boxes onto a shelf, and one slipped. Patrick called out for Therese's help. He could see the back of her blonde ponytail, but

she did not turn around. He asked again. Without her help, he shoved the boxes onto the shelf and went to find her. She disappeared, but a cold feeling lingered where he saw her. Patrick left the storeroom.

He found Therese in the cafeteria wiping down the salad bar. Patrick asked why she had not come over to help him. It was clear she had been cleaning the salad bar the whole time. That's when Patrick noticed: Therese was wearing her hair down—*not* in a ponytail. Five other people had the same story about seeing "her" in the storeroom.

The cooking staff reports a different lady, a nun, in a back tunnel. No one will go alone to take the garbage out because they all get scared in the hallway to the tunnel. The cafeteria staff swear a dead nun is the ghost haunting that tunnel. The tunnel is dark and feels gloomy. Imagine running into her in the dark.

Holy Cross Hospital is still a busy place. But when the call lights flash in Rooms 117 or 118, the nurses know not to worry, the nuns will take care of it.

CHAPTER 8

Gentleman Ghosts

The Alta Club for men is at the beginning of South Temple. South Temple in the early days was Salt Lake City's Grand Boulevard, where the wealthiest Utahns lived or worked. The gentlemen's club was established in 1883 to serve those who came west to get rich and wanted to enjoy what the Latter-day Saints people did not: drinking, smoking, and gambling. One thing is for sure, the club is very protective of its members, including its ghosts. The best way to learn about them is in a roundabout way.

Two boys were playing ball when they heard a distinctive CRASH. They looked at each other and then at the mug lying beside their ball. It was a family heirloom.

Coming around the corner, their mother scolded, "How many times have I told you two not to play ball in the house?"

Picking up the mug, mom began, "You are lucky this didn't break. This was Great-Uncle Pete's Alta Club mug. If your father finds it broken, he might let you boys go join the ghosts of the club."

"Did you say there are ghosts at the Alta Club?" Jed asked. "Are there really?"

"Yes, according to Uncle Pete," mom replied.

"What happens? Who are they? Can we go see them?" Adam wondered.

"Slow down my little Ghostbusters," mom responded. "You'll need to ask your dad. He's the one whose ancestors settled this place."

When their dad walked through the door, they badgered him with questions about the Alta Club ghosts.

Confused, he held up his hands in self-defense. "Whoa, whoa, whoa! Where did all this come from?" he questioned.

"We were playing ball in the house and knocked over your Alta Club mug. Mom got mad and said if we broke it you would kill us and we would be ghosts at the club," Jed answered.

Dad laughed. "Well, I probably wouldn't kill you. Disappointed, maybe. Your Great-Uncle Pete gave that to me, and it reminds me of him and all his stories."

"Yeah, yeah, but what about the ghosts?" they wanted to know.

Dad began, "We will get there. First, let me tell you a little about the Alta Club. It began as a club for business executives who wanted to gather after work, unwind, drink, smoke, play cards. You could order food and there were rooms to stay in if someone was from out of town. Uncle Pete was a young, successful business owner. The club wanted younger members, so they invited him to join.

"The younger men were soon being referred to as the 'Boy Scouts,' not because of their good deeds but because they were younger, loud, and rambunctious. Older members complained about their loudness. The manager moved them to the lower level so if they were noisy it would not bother the older members. Uncle Pete enjoyed boasting that the Grill Room was the creation of the Boy Scouts."

"Are the ghosts in the Grill Room then?" Adam asked.

"No, just the opposite. That is where they are not. The ghosts are upstairs. Uncle Pete talked about ghost sightings in the main library. It began when a longtime member had gone missing. The police began a weeklong search, finally finding the man dead in his favorite leather chair in the library. No one knew how long he had been there. Pete never knew if the story was true but admitted that the library always felt a bit unsettling, like someone was watching you, and occasionally the rocking chairs would rock all by themselves."

"Do you think the dead guy's ghost is in the library?" Adam asked.

"Maybe," dad replied. "The other story Uncle Pete told me about happened years later. He cautioned that booze, smoking, and sleep are a poor combination.

"One night after a long workday, a member stopped at the club for a few drinks. He felt too tired to go home, so he asked for a room. Once in his room, he enjoyed his expensive cigar before bed. He was sleepy. The booze made him sleepier, and he drifted off, dropping the cigar on the rug, where it slowly smoldered into a fire. It engulfed the room with smoke and flames. Then it spread.

Everyone escaped the fire except for him. He died and never left. They say that man still walks the upper floors checking the rooms to make sure that no one else falls asleep smoking."

"Who was he?" Adam asked.

Dad replied, "I don't know. When I asked Uncle Pete, all he would say was, 'He paid the price of his carelessness with his life. Let's let him rest in peace.'"

"Does anything else happen?" Jed asked.

"I have heard that sometimes members will feel someone touch them on their shoulders. They turn but no one is there."

"That's creepy," Jed said. "Have you ever been to the Alta Club?"

"Yes, Uncle Pete took me a few times."

"Did you see any ghosts?" Adam asked.

"No, but I noticed the smell of lilacs," dad responded. "I thought that was strange. It is a gentlemen's club, so you'd expect to smell cigars, not flowers. Ghost lore says that when you smell lilac or lavender in a building, a ghost is nearby. I didn't see them, but I knew they were there."

CHAPTER 9

A Walk with the Dead

The City-County Building was built on South State Street on the ten-acre block of Washington Square Park. Originally called Emigration Square, it was the place where the first pioneers camped when entering the valley. The building is unique, and has a labyrinth of underground tunnels that go to the old jail where the Main Library now stands. Built by the Freemasons and dedicated in 1893, it was meant to rival the Salt Lake City Temple.

The ghost tour bus pulled down the tree-lined circle and stopped in front of the massive, statuesque City-County Building, which rises three hundred feet to a bell tower. Though it was dark out, the guides pointed out the stone carvings with gargoyles, animals, roses, people, and past events in Utah's history.

The guides began sharing ghostly encounters when a security guard interrupted them. Nervous, they left the bus to explain why they were there. It delighted them to discover the guard, Bill Conway, was a paranormal fan, and he invited the guides to return at the end of the evening's tour to swap stories.

They returned, and he gave them a tour. Bill explained that he liked the graveyard shift. Ghosts didn't bother him. He enjoyed keeping track of them. Which was a good thing, because the building has quite a few! One of Bill's favorite stories was from a previous guard.

The guard was walking the floors when the elevator opened. A distinguished older man exited. They nodded a greeting. The man continued down the hall carrying a cane and dressed formally in a top hat and tails. The guard dismissed the odd clothing. City officials often attend special parties all dressed up. But when the guard took a second glance, no one was there. The man had vanished.

This troubled him. The man looked familiar, but who was he? He reviewed building employees but was drawing a blank. Frustrated, he continued his rounds. On the third floor, he passed the portrait of former Salt Lake City mayor R.N. Baskin—the building's first mayor.

He glanced at the portrait, then did a double-take. He stopped and stared; it hit him! The portrait was of the same man who greeted him at the elevator—the ghost of long-deceased R.N. Baskin! The gossip was true: Mayor Baskin watches over his beloved building.

The guides had heard stories about children being in the building and wondered what Bill knew. Bill shared one story of the ghostly children playing in the restroom on the fourth floor, bothering an employee.

Beatrice was an executive assistant. She was stern, serious, and didn't have time for goofing around. She followed the rules and didn't like those who disobeyed.

One afternoon, escaping to the employee restroom, she checked to make sure she was alone. It didn't take long before the giggling voices of children playing around interrupted her. She was mad and burst out of the stall, yelling. "You children get out of here. You have no business being in here. How did you get in here, anyway?"

The room was empty. One by one, she opened the stalls, continuing to yell. "We reserve this restroom for employees. You don't belong here. This is a place of business."

She found no one. Exasperated, she washed and left—only to hear a ball bouncing down the stairs. That was too much. This was not a playground. She wanted those kids gone. She called security, insisting they remove the pesky children.

Security doubted they would find anything, but they searched anyway. Some wonder how the children came to inhabit the building. During the building's construction, signs warned "Danger—Keep Out." But a brother and sister ignored the signs and snuck in. While exploring, a board broke; they fell down a shaft and didn't survive the fall. They died here and now see it as their playground.

The guides asked about rumors of a bride or a mother. Did he have any ideas?

Bill did. He confirmed there was a woman ghost. But reports of a jilted bride or the mother of the phantom children never made sense to him, the mother being grief stricken, the bride heartbroken. The womanly accounts were never sad; they were of a busy woman. He wondered who it might be. Then one quiet evening, thinking about her, he stopped. Suddenly, in the stillness, he felt a presence, something, brush by him. He listened. It was faint, like fabric dragging on the ground, like the swish of a full skirt—then clicking heels hurried down the hall. He looked and noticed he was standing next to Room 335, the room dedicated to Martha Hughes Cannon. It wasn't a mother or a bride, it was Dr. Cannon, continuing her work.

The guides asked where the ghosts were most active.

Bill didn't hesitate. The third floor, where one room was a portal—a passageway between worlds. He even had proof. One night while doing rounds, he walked into the corner office on the northeast side and noticed it was freezing. Grabbing his phone, he quickly took a picture. It did not surprise him when he printed the photo: there was a distinct shadowy figure in the picture that he had not seen. He had the guides follow him to his office, where he gave them a copy of the picture. It had been featured in the newspaper. They all agreed it was one of the most haunted buildings in Salt Lake City.

CHAPTER 10

Pesky Poltergeist

Albert and Elizabeth McCune built their home on a hillside with a view of the capitol building for Alfred and the Salt Lake Temple for Elizabeth. Finished in 1901, it is a three-story, twenty-one-room bungalow-style mansion. Alfred built it for Elizabeth, sparing no expense in granting her heart's desire, including the large ballroom mirror shipped in one piece from Germany. The house has had a variety of occupants, but its beauty and structure remain timeless. Very little has changed.

The McCunes lived in the home for twenty years. Instead of selling their beloved home, they donated the mansion to The Church of the Latter-day Saints. It became the McCune School of Music and Art, then the Virginia Tanner Modern Dance School. Finally, Philip McCarthey purchased it in 1999, renovating and updating it. Since then, we have known it as the McCune Mansion—Salt Lake City's wedding and business event center. The McCune Mansion event center motto is "to provide a historic treasure which embodies fine taste, gracious hospitality, and superb service," with the unwritten promise of so much more. It is good to know that if you host an event at the mansion, you may encounter some additional items that are not advertised.

Sandra loved working for the McCune Mansion event center. The mansion was breathtaking, filled with rare beauty like an Egytian marble fireplace, hand-painted ceilings, gold-leaf gilding, exquisite murals, and more. It made decorating easy. She put the finishing touches on the table preparations.

Suddenly, a loud, long scream disrupted her peaceful moment. Sandra quickly moved towards the terrifying noise and collided with Colleen, another employee.

"What's wrong?" she asked.

Grabbing Sandra's wrist, Colleen dragged Sandra into the spacious drawing room. On one wall was a large picture of young ballerinas, all dressed in white. The girl in front was on her toes. Across the room was a full-sized wall mirror. Colleen pointed at the large mirror and stammered. "I was lighting candles when something caught my eye. I turned and watched a young girl in a flowing white dress come out of the mirror!" Shaking, she repeated, "She came out of the mirror and then disappeared. I looked around the room, trying to find her. She vanished. I could swear that it was the same girl in that picture there." She pointed to the large mural of ballerinas. "The one with blonde hair. It was her, I swear."

"Okay," Sandra said, pulling out a chair, "why don't you sit down for a second and I'll go get you some water."

Colleen muttered to herself, "I don't think it was the lights. Maybe it was. I don't want to believe in ghosts, but what else could it be? It was real. Something was there!"

Sandra returned with the water and sat down to comfort Colleen. Before she said anything, Colleen burst out, "You act like it is nothing, but something moves things in this house. This place has unseen guests. I am not making this stuff up. Strange things happen here."

Sandra patiently responded, "No one is saying you are making anything up. I believe you."

"You do?" said Colleen.

Sandra continued, "I do. Not everyone is sensitive enough to experience what is here. I wait before I say anything because I don't want to freak people out. Yeah, there are unseen guests. The first sightings came shortly after the music school moved in. Music played, but there were no musicians. Elizabeth had a secret room built for musicians to play at her parties, but they were long gone.

"You met our ballerina ghost. Her footsteps will show up in the carpet and then disappear."

When Philip McCarthey first renovated the place, his family had Christmas here. It was a glorious celebration until Phil sent his daughters to turn off the upstairs ballroom lights. They couldn't find the switch. Phil tried and couldn't find it, either. He noticed the portrait of Alfred McCune and wondered if Alfred was mad that the great-grandson of Thomas Kearns, Alfred's rival in politics, was now claiming his home as well. Phil reassured him he only had good intentions. Still unable to turn the lights out, he hollered, "Okay, Mr. McCune, you win!" The lights flickered but stayed on. It was a few days later that an electrician found the problem, probably because by then Alfred and Phil had somehow made peace.

Colleen asked, "Is there a ghost in the kitchen?"

Sandra laughed, "There sure is. Chris, the head chef, has many stories of watching new employees during their first encounter with the ghost. He will show them something when a pot crashes to the ground, or a bowl will move on its own and everyone ignores it."

The new hire will finally ask with panic in their voice, "did you not see that bowl float down the counter?"

Then the group will laugh. "Yes, we saw it," Chris will reply calmly. "We were just waiting to see if you would admit to seeing it."

Sandra continued, "If you are uncomfortable with the supernatural, then you may not like it here. But if you can get comfortable with uninvited guests, you will be okay."

Colleen thought, then admitted, "I guess if I am not the only one seeing things I can handle it."

The mansion continues to host the most romantic, beautiful, and memorable events. If you enjoy the unexpected, you may think of having your next big event there as well.

STATE OF UTAH

CHAPTER 11

Are You All Right?

The Utah State Capitol sits on a hill to the north of Salt Lake City. It looks just like the US Capitol. In 1906, Edward and Minnette Woodruff built a stylish mansion, now a bed-and-breakfast called the Inn on the Hill, on a corner just below the capitol.

Summer walked down the stairs of the Inn on the Hill to the front desk and flopped into her chair. The front desk was at the back of the mansion-turned-bed-and-breakfast. Sometimes there was a lot of running up and down stairs.

She had the perfect job for a student. Not a lot of stress plus time to study.

Her job at the inn was simple: keep guests happy. She cleaned, answered phones, and ran to the storage room for supplies.

The storage room was creepy. It was in the attic of the old mansion.

The rest of the mansion was fine. For the rest of it, she felt love.

A portrait of Edward and Minnette Woodruff hung near the reception desk. Edward was tall and thin, while Minnette was shorter and had a beautiful smile.

After Minnette's cancer diagnosis, her husband, Edward, took care of her as she lay dying. Their large room, with a cozy fireplace and small bay window, was on the second floor of the building. Every fifteen minutes he would stand over her bed and ask, "Are you all right? Do you need anything?"

Now, people who stay in that room say that a nice man stood over their bed and asked, "Are you all right? Do you need anything?"

Don't you wonder why people don't scream at him to get out? How do you think you would respond?

Apparently, they think he is so kind and charming. They appreciate him. The staff does not mention the ghost.

It was Summer's turn to get supplies from the attic again. She was out of the extra toilet paper she usually stashed behind the desk to avoid extra trips to the attic.

She would try to get in and out as fast as humanly possible.

Summer placed the skeleton key in the storage room lock and turned it.

The door stuck. People were arriving. She did not have time for this.

She pulled hard. The door did not budge. She ran to get Staci, another hostess.

Did she need help or just another person? The eerie feeling consumed her.

The two women pulled on the door together. One of them even had both feet up on the wall for leverage! Nothing would make that door budge.

The owner arrived and came upstairs, a bit bewildered by the commotion.

They explained they would have to get a locksmith or an ax to open the old door. The owner sighed, walking over to the door. She said it was a pity to harm the old door when it had such great charm.

As she touched the key, the door sprang open. The owner looked around. The employees looked stunned. That door was stuck only minutes before!

The owner raised her eyebrows and invited them to get ready for the guests.

The attic was strange, but the basement was worse. The Woodruff mansion was built on a hill, so it was not like most old basements. It was still creepy.

Summer felt like someone watched her when she was in the basement. Once she thought she heard someone come downstairs into the room she was cleaning.

She asked if someone forgot something. Nothing.

Summer turned around. No one was there, but she distinctly felt someone enter the room. She checked upstairs. Not one soul had entered.

Despite her fear of the creepy attic and dismal basement, she was fine in the rest of the house.

Ghost hunters always seem to show up at haunted buildings. They want to check for ghosts with their professional equipment.

Staci, however never wanted to know what they found. Staci was pregnant and felt uneasy about ghosts. So that day, she offered to make treats before she left the building.

Summer let the ghost hunters set up recording equipment by her desk.

She invited them to have coffee and cookies and worked upstairs that night.

Can you believe not a single ghost appeared while they were there? Their EVP (electronic voice phenomenon) recorded every sound.

They found nothing—until they replayed the recording.

The ghost hunters sat, waiting for something to happen. It appeared the ghosts had been sitting around waiting, too.

"Who made the coffee? It's good," one of ghost hunters asked.

No one answered him.

Yet, on the recording, a whispering voice replied, "Staci did."

After ghost hunters gave their report to the owner and staff members, all agreed, “Don’t tell Staci!” The ghost knew her name!

The next day, as Summer vacuumed the stairs, she thought about the stories from the inn.

She felt a sudden surge of love. Looking up, she saw movement in the room’s doorway on the left.

There was the silhouette of a tall, thin man hugging a woman. The lights were off in the room, but something cast that shadow onto the door. No one checked into the room.

Summer knew she had just witnessed a special moment.

She smiled, understanding the true charm of this old place. That feeling of pure, devoted love drew many others to the Inn on the Hill.

When walking by the door of that room, Summer could almost hear the words, “Are you all right? Do you need anything?”

The Paranormal Purple Lady

Brijma shuddered, stepping out of the ladies' restroom into the corridor. Earlier, on her way into the ladies' room, a strange crowd standing around had stunned her.

The people in the crowd looked disconnected and lost. And their clothing was odd. Men, women, and children wearing fashions from the latter 1800s to the mid-1900s.

Wondering if they were actors, Brijma slipped by them as fast as she could into the welcome vacancy of the ladies' room.

Her heart pounded and her washed hands were sweaty as she reached for the door. Stepping into the passageway, her hair stood on end. She turned and walked sideways to squeeze through the even more crowded hallway. Reaching her table in the Rio Grande Café, her hand trembled as she reached for her water. Her lunch companion, Ave, noted her pale complexion.

"What a peculiar crowd; look how they're dressed. Why do you think they gathered in the corridor like that?" Eyeing them once again, Brijma whispered, "They give me the creeps."

"What crowd?" Ave replied, glancing in the restroom's direction and continuing her meal.

Waving for the server, Brijma inquired about the eerie throng assembled. "I don't see anyone. It's been a slow day," the server smiled, setting the check onto the table.

Without glancing at the check, and vowing to never return, Brijma dropped a couple of twenties onto the table. Then ran out of the building, leaving Ave and the server mystified.

Perhaps the mysterious otherworldly guests understood a train will get them somewhere, anywhere, even if they are unsure where that is. To catch a train, you go to the depot.

In 1910, they completed the Denver & Rio Grande Depot in all its splendor. This train depot staged farewells and homecomings of soldiers and families in World War I and World War II, because Salt Lake City was considered the crossroads of the West.

World War II created the need to transport large numbers of soldiers. Fifteen to twenty trains filled with service people passed through the depot daily.

But once the war ended, that many people weren't traveling to the Denver & Rio Grande Depot anymore. After falling into disrepair, the building was sold to the State of Utah for $1.

The state then restored the depot to its former glory. Today it is home to history, arts, records, a restaurant, and ghosts!

Gloria Simmons was in love. She counted down the days until Orton, her soldier serving in World War II, returned home.

The big day came. He was to arrive by train at the depot.

Gloria wore her favorite purple dress. She put on a purple pillbox hat with a slight veil of purple tulle. Her raven-colored hair was styled to perfection.

Gloria reached the depot early. She wanted to be the first person he saw. She waited on the platform, holding her breath as each train pulled into the station.

Their moment arrived. In rolled a passenger car full of uniformed young men. Her soldier leaped from the train before it even came to a complete stop.

The young lovers rushed into each other's arms,

enveloping themselves in a fond embrace. Gloria chattered, catching him up on everything while he had been away. Her sister was going to have a baby, and her best friend, Peggy, got engaged. She expressed the fun she had hosting dances for the soldiers.

Orton wanted to know what dances she helped host.

Gloria described the dances held for the soldiers coming in on the trains and layovers. She was sure she told him about the dances in her letters. Gloria mentioned the poor soldier to whom she was writing. She felt sorry he had received no letters while he was away.

The lovebirds quarreled. One thing led to another, and Gloria took off her engagement ring and shoved the ring into Orton's hand.

Not to be outmaneuvered, he

impulsively threw the ring. It landed on the rails.

Without looking, she jumped onto the tracks to retrieve the ring, and an oncoming train struck her.

She has remained at the station since that fateful day. Her apparition appears in the ladies' restroom near the Rio Grande Café.

Rhonda was washing her hands in one of the six sinks forming an island in the center of the ladies' room. She noticed the reflection of a striking woman in the mirror across from her. She smiled politely, musing about the woman's unusual demeanor and clothing. The lady wore a purple old-fashioned dress. Her pillbox hat gave her a peculiar purple glow through the tulle veil. The stranger in the mirror stared at her with deep sadness. A chill ran down Rhonda's spine. She turned to get a better look and properly greet the woman. But when Rhonda looked where the purplish lady was standing, no one was there!

A server at the café had an equally puzzling experience. While washing her hands in the ladies' room, she sensed she was not alone. She caught a glance of a lady adorned in purple reflected in the mirror. Each of the antique sinks, with separate hot and cold faucets, turned on by themselves. One at a time, each sink spewed water, hot then cold, and then on to the next sink. The toilets joined in the cacophony, flushing one at a time. When she recovered from her fright, she rushed out the room, never to return without a coworker.

The legend of the young sweethearts has been passed down for decades and is part of the common lore. A psychic revealed the names of the couple, Gloria Simmons and Orton.

There is a twist to the story, however. In 2002, ghost hunters set up recording equipment, and on playback, they heard a voice whispering, "He pushed me!"

CHAPTER 13

Larry Meets Charlie

In the middle of South Temple sits a grand Egyptian-styled building. Egyptians are known for being great builders. So are Freemasons. Both use symbols in architecture. Two sphinx flank the steps at the Masonic Temple. They say, under a full moon the sphinx might tell your fortune.

Sometimes lights on the building flicker. What would you think if you saw a person standing in the window of this locked and empty building? In the 1930s, a ghost named Charlie moved into the Masonic Temple.

Long ago, Larry Fairclough hurried up the steps looking for Linda, his dance partner for the evening. They heard their friends talking about going ghost hunting upstairs. The group turned and hurried out of the room.

They ran, then crept up two flights of stairs. They wandered down a hallway. After taking a few slow steps down the hall—BAM!

A slamming door sent the group running in every direction. Everyone agreed: Charlie the ghost made the dance even better.

That night at the dance, Larry had no idea one day he would again cross paths with the Masonic Temple—and Charlie.

Years later, Larry began a career in construction and joined the Freemasons. Their secret meetings and handshakes, as well as their use of symbolism—hidden in plain sight—was intriguing to Larry.

Over the years, he heard people talk about experiences with the trickster ghost, but he did not have any.

Charlie had been dead since the late 1920s. He spent so much time at the lodge in life that his widow said to send him back there when he died.

Charlie's ashes sat on a mantel, were moved to a bookcase, then stowed on a storage shelf until they were forgotten. About then, a man fitting Charlie's description began appearing.

Strange things began happening at the lodge. Lights turned on and off, doors opened and closed, and furniture and decorations moved.

Larry had been around for years, but he still had no proof of Charlie.

Trina was Larry's niece. Her husband, Ray, got a job as the night watchman at the temple. They lived in the basement and watched over the Masonic Temple at night. (The rent-free basement apartment went with the job.)

One night, Ray finished locking up. He heard banging noises, and lights turned on by themselves.

Ray called the police. He explained that someone broke in, but the person on the other end of the phone did not seem suprised hearing this was the Masonic Temple. Perhaps he received similar phone calls before?

The officer told Ray they would send a car to check the perimeter.

Ray felt stunned. He and Trina checked the building. There was no one there.

The next morning, Ray talked to the manager, Dave, who already seemed to know what had happened.

He guessed that lights went on and off and that there was banging. He even seemed to know about the police not believing they needed to come.

Ray seemed surprised that Dave had not told him. Dave just laughed.

Do you think Ray and Trina would have taken the job had they known they would live with a ghost? Would you?

Charlie always found a way to startle Ray and Trina. They moved out as soon as possible.

You will not believe what happened next. In 1985, during a major cleaning and remodeling project, they found Charlie's ashes! The legend was true, now they had proof!

Can you believe it took two more years before Larry met Charlie himself?

It was a Sunday evening. As an adult leader, Larry was helping the boys put on a play.

After everyone went home, Larry was in the main hall, alone.

Then the chairs started flipping. Someone was walking down a row and flipped four of the chairs. Larry could see no one.

It startled him at first, but Larry did not feel afraid.

He had locked the doors himself when everyone left. He asked if anyone was there. No answer.

Larry walked into the hallway to check. No one. As he walked back into the room, he knew he was not alone.

He called out that they were just trying to raise money.

Larry locked up and went home. Charlie could have the place to himself.

What would have upset Charlie so much?

In 1993, Larry became Grand Master. He wondered if Brother Charlie wanted a funeral?

The fraternity owned some cemetery plots. They held a lovely service to help Brother Charlie feel celebrated.

They opened the west doors for the Master Mason's funeral. What would happen to their ghost?

No activity for eight months. People kept telling Charlie stories. The Masonic family missed him. Larry felt sad.

Larry wondered if he did the right thing. The Masonic Temple was the place that made Charlie happy. Larry wished he were back.

Then the elevator seized up and would not move. An elevator repairman came to the rescue.

A bright light was bleeding through the crack of the elevator doors. The elevator repairman could find nothing wrong with it. The light made no sense.

Suddenly, the elevator shone wild and bright. The elevator doors released and opened! The light inside exploded, then faded to normal.

Master Larry just smiled at Charlie's dramatic return to the Masonic Temple.

Laurie B. Allen has been interested in ghost stories since she was a child. She has been a story-guide with Ogden and Salt Lake City Ghost Tours since it began and enjoys the thrill of telling the stories of actual hauntings.

Cassie Howard-Ashton believes ghost stories are a great tool to teach children how to deal with fearful feelings and the unexplainable. She loves telling, teaching, writing, and inspiring others with stories. Cassie lives with her adorable and supportive husband and large family in Salt Lake City, Utah.

Kristen Clay is the creator and director of Story Tours: Ogden and SLC Ghost Tours, Hysterical History Tours, and custom storytelling concerts. She is known for bringing various cultures alive to audiences around the world. Kristen currently lives in Utah with her cat, Mei Mei and her part-time stray visitor, Muggsy the Murder Cat.

Nannette Guest-Watts was born in a haunted hospital in Los Angeles, California, and was afraid of ghosts until she started learning the stories and legends in Salt Lake City. She serves on the Timpanogos Storytelling Festival committee as director of National Youth Storytelling. Nannette lives at the base of a canyon surrounded by large mountains, where she raised six children with her husband.

Check out some of the other Spooky America titles available now!

Spooky America was adapted from the creeptastic Haunted America series for adults. Haunted America explores historical haunts in cities and regions across America. Each book chronicles both the widely known and less-familiar history behind local ghosts and other unexplained mysteries. Here's more from the *Haunted Salt Lake City* authors: